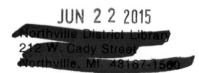

Jason DERULO

Joanne Mattern

Mitchell Lane
PUBLISHERS
P.O. Box 196
Hockessin, Delaware 19707
Visit us on the web: www.mitchelllane.com
Comments? E-mail us: mitchelllane@mitchelllane.com

Printing   1   2   3   4   5   6   7   8   9

Blue Banner Biographies

Abby Wambach	Ice Cube	Miguel Tejada
Adele	Ja Rule	Mike Trout
Alicia Keys	Jamie Foxx	Nancy Pelosi
Allen Iverson	Jason Derulo	Natasha Bedingfield
Ashanti	Jay-Z	Nicki Minaj
Ashlee Simpson	Jennifer Hudson	One Direction
Ashton Kutcher	Jennifer Lopez	Orianthi
Avril Lavigne	Jessica Simpson	Orlando Bloom
Blake Lively	J. K. Rowling	P. Diddy
Blake Shelton	Joe Flacco	Peyton Manning
Bow Wow	John Legend	Pink
Brett Favre	Justin Berfield	Pit Bull
Britney Spears	Justin Timberlake	Prince William
Bruno Mars	Kanye West	Queen Latifah
CC Sabathia	Kate Hudson	Rihanna
Carrie Underwood	Katy Perry	Robert Downey Jr.
Chris Brown	Keith Urban	Robert Pattinson
Chris Daughtry	Kelly Clarkson	Ron Howard
Christina Aguilera	Kenny Chesney	Sean Kingston
Ciara	Ke$ha	Selena
Clay Aiken	Kevin Durant	Shakira
Cole Hamels	Kristen Stewart	Shia LaBeouf
Condoleezza Rice	Lady Gaga	Shontelle Layne
Corbin Bleu	Lance Armstrong	Soulja Boy Tell 'Em
Daniel Radcliffe	Leona Lewis	Stephenie Meyer
David Ortiz	Lil Wayne	Taylor Swift
David Wright	Lionel Messi	T.I.
Derek Jeter	Lindsay Lohan	Timbaland
Drew Brees	LL Cool J	Tim McGraw
Eminem	Ludacris	Tim Tebow
Eve	Mariah Carey	Toby Keith
Fergie	Mario	Usher
Flo Rida	Mary J. Blige	Vanessa Anne Hudgens
Gwen Stefani	Mary-Kate and Ashley Olsen	Will.i.am
Hope Solo	Megan Fox	Zac Efron

Library of Congress Cataloging-in-Publication Data
Mattern, Joanne, 1963–
 Jason Derulo / by Joanne Mattern.
     pages cm. — (Blue banner biographies)
 Includes bibliographical references and index.
 ISBN 978-1-61228-643-3 (library bound)
 1. Derulo, Jason, 1989– —Juvenile literature. 2. Singers—United States—Biography—Juvenile literature. I. Title.
 ML3930.D427M37 2014
 782.42164092—dc23
 [B]
                                                                      2014023697
eBook ISBN: 9781612286679

ABOUT THE AUTHOR: Joanne Mattern is the author of many books for children. She specializes in nonfiction and especially likes writing about people and animals. Joanne has written many books for Mitchell Lane, including biographies as well as several books about food and culture. She lives in New York State with her husband, children, and several pets.

PUBLISHER'S NOTE: The following story has been thoroughly researched, and to the best of our knowledge represents a true story. While every possible effort has been made to ensure accuracy, the publisher will not assume liability for damages caused by inaccuracies in the data and makes no warranty on the accuracy of the information contained herein. This story has not been authorized or endorsed by Jason Derulo.

Blue Banner Biography

Derulo wows the crowd in an unusual outfit during a performance at the World Music Awards in Monte Carlo on May 27, 2014.

A Frightening Moment

Jason Derulo was on top of the world. It was January 3, 2012, and the singer was rehearsing the stage show for his upcoming Future History world tour. Derulo enjoyed dancing and performing acrobatic stunts onstage. He wanted to do more than just sing for his fans. "For my show I want to bring a performance-art element," he told MTV News before the rehearsal. "It won't just be a run-of-the-mill me standing in front of the band. It will be a lot of dancing, obviously, but there will be somewhat of a story line, almost like a musical."

However, Derulo's plans changed dramatically on that January day. As he was trying to jump and tumble forward, he accidentally landed on his neck. Derulo knew he was badly hurt. An ambulance rushed him to Memorial West Hospital in Pembroke Pines, Florida. There Derulo received the bad news. He had fractured a vertebra in his neck. Doctors told him he was lucky he wasn't paralyzed.

Derulo tried to keep his sense of humor, especially when he told his fans about the accident. "I fractured my neck doing tumbling and acrobatics 4 tour!" he tweeted to his fans, along with a photo of him lying in bed with a

Derulo did not let his serious accident get him down. During 2012 he was often photographed wearing fancy gear such as the rhinestone-encrusted neck brace he wore to a concert in Los Angeles.

heavy brace around his injured neck. "Always tryin 2 push boundaries 4 YOU!" Then he added a joke. Referring to his neck brace, Derulo asked, "Like my new chain?"

Derulo was optimistic, but the truth was that the accident was a huge setback. Derulo had to cancel his entire tour, along with all promotional appearances. He also had to wear the neck brace for several months to make sure he healed completely. Derulo knew his fans were disappointed, and he was upset as well.

"It was the craziest thing that ever happened in my life," Derulo later told a reporter from the *Daily Record*, a British newspaper. "It was a horrifying experience, but the recovery process just changed my life, because I grew up as a man. I was pretty much humbled by the whole thing, due to not being able to do the simple things by myself, like tie my shoelaces or take a shower. It opened my eyes to what matters in life and just who matters, like my family, who were always there for me. I came out on top."

> In spite of the setback, Derulo refused to stay down for long. During his recovery, he wrote more than 300 songs.

In spite of the setback, Derulo refused to stay down for long. During his recovery, he wrote more than 300 songs. As soon as he could, he went into the studio and recorded almost 120 of the new songs. Some of those tracks appeared on his next album, *Tattoos*, which was released on September 24, 2013. Even before that, Derulo was back onstage performing. It seemed that nothing could keep this master of song and dance down for long.

Derulo often lends his talents to help other performers. He took part in the Grammy SoundChecks program, part of the Grammy In the Schools interactive music education program.

CHAPTER 2

Born to Sing and Dance

Jason Joel Desrouleaux was born on September 21, 1989, in Miami, Florida. His family was originally from Haiti. Even though his parents were not very interested in the arts, Derulo has loved music as long as he can remember. "My only musical influence—as I was growing up—was school and television, because I didn't have anybody in my household that sang or did any kind of performing at all!" he told *Blues and Soul* in 2009. "So for me, it all really came from the inside. I just always had this desire to sing and perform."

Family and friends soon came to expect that Derulo would entertain any time there was a family get-together. Derulo grew up with lots of cousins, so, "There was always a birthday!" he told *Blues and Soul*. "And so I'd be singing and dancing at every family function. . . . I just continued doing it for years and years."

Even though Jason's parents weren't musical themselves, they encouraged Jason's talent. When he was eight years old, Jason enrolled in a local performing arts school. As he grew up, he studied theater, opera, and ballet.

Derulo got a lot of experience performing in musical theater productions, such as the hit shows *Smokey Joe's Cafe* and *Ragtime*. Derulo found those experiences to be extremely valuable to his later career. He says that in musical theater, "the whole storyline is explained through the song. With musical theater, every word becomes so vivid, because you have to see everything. And I have really tried to translate that into my own songwriting as well. I always want the audience to actually see what's going on in the song."

Derulo also became a gifted songwriter. He wrote his first song when he was only eight years old. It was about his crush on a girl he knew.

Studying so many different types of performing arts also helped Jason develop his own unique style as he got older, although he didn't realize that at first. "I've studied music my whole life, so it's not something that just popped out of nowhere yesterday," Derulo told *Beatweek* magazine in 2010. "I study all kinds of music. . . . I love it all. So I wanted to make music that way. . . . Why do I have to do one specific kind of music? I went through many stages in what kind of performer I wanted to be. . . . So it took me awhile to kind of find myself and realize that I didn't have to choose one. I could just make music, and whatever came out would just be me."

Derulo also became a gifted songwriter. He wrote his first song when he was only eight years old. It was about his crush on a girl he knew. "I started songwriting because I felt I needed to express myself," Derulo told *Blues and Soul*. At that time, Derulo was studying classical music, and he

Derulo poses with fellow international superstar Pitbull backstage at a Jingle Ball concert in Dallas, Texas, on December 2, 2013.

found that performing songs written by others made him feel annoyed. "When you're doing classical music everything has to be sung the way it's written. That became really uncomfortable for me." His teachers often scolded him for "ruining" a song by changing the way it was sung. "So at eight I just took things into my own hands and wrote this song called 'Crush On You' for this girl called Amy," he confessed. "Then from there I just kept writing every single day."

By the time he was sixteen years old, Derulo was writing songs for major rap and hip-hop artists such as P. Diddy, Sean Kingston, Pitbull, Lil Wayne, and Danity Kane. Derulo enjoyed writing songs, but he really wanted to be onstage performing them himself. All he needed was someone to give him his big break.

Producer J.R. Rotem was an invaluable help in launching Derulo's career. The two have worked together since 2006 and have won many awards, including the BMI Pop Awards.

CHAPTER 3

The Big Time

*I*n 2006, Derulo graduated from the American Musical and Dramatic Academy, a well-known school in New York City. That year was a big one for Derulo in other ways as well. He won the grand prize on the television show *Showtime at the Apollo*. This show spotlighted singers and dancers who performed at New York City's legendary Apollo Theater.

Soon afterward, Derulo met a music producer named J.R. Rotem. Rotem liked what he saw. He signed Derulo to his record label, Beluga Heights Records, which was part of Warner Brothers Records. "Jason Derulo has one of the most impressive work ethics I've ever come across--he just keeps knocking out songs in the studio," Rotem told *HitQuarters* in 2010. "That's an amazing quality."

Derulo worked with Rotem for several years. Finally, in 2009, Derulo released his first single. It was called "Whatcha Say." The song was an instant hit. Just a few weeks after it was released, "Whatcha Say" entered the *Billboard* Hot 100 chart at number 54. In November, the song hit number one. Derulo also released a music video for the song, which became popular on YouTube.

Since his first single was doing so well, Derulo went into the studio to record an album. Before the album came out, Derulo released a single from it on December 8. Titled "In My Head," the song rose to number five on the *Billboard* Hot 100 and became a popular song on the radio that winter and spring.

On March 2, 2010, Derulo's first album, *Jason Derulo*, was released. The album wasn't just popular in the United States. It rose into the top ten of the British and Irish music charts as well. Two other singles, "Ridin' Solo" and "What If," also moved into top ten positions on the charts.

Derulo worked very hard to make his first album. He went to the studio and worked twenty-hour days to record three hundred songs. Derulo's goal was to release an album that included his best possible music. He also wanted to make sure his songs did not sound the same. Derulo recorded many different styles, including hip-hop, pop, ballads, and rhythm and blues, or R&B. As he told *Beatweek*, "I reinvent myself on each song. You can't really get to know somebody after one song."

Derulo also wanted to break down the barriers between what listeners thought of as "black" music and "white" music. He wanted to attract fans of all different races who didn't care if he was black or white. Derulo believed that people should just enjoy music and that skin color should never be an issue.

Like most artists, Derulo knew that going on tour was a great way to let fans hear his new album, and fans were eager to see this rising star. Derulo signed on as the opening act for Lady Gaga's Monster Ball Tour. Lady Gaga was hugely popular and her tour was a complex show filled with different types of performances. Derulo found the experience amazing and exciting, although he was nervous about opening for such a big star. "She forced me to step my game up," Derulo told MTV. "I have to go in there with my

The 2010 Teen Choice Awards showed just how popular Derulo was with young audiences. Derulo won two awards that night and had a lot of fun appearing on the show.

game face on. The audiences have just been incredible, and I can't wait to do my own tour." Derulo also found a friend in Lady Gaga herself. One night she told Derulo he was special. "That meant a lot to me coming from her," he told *Beatweek* magazine.

Derulo's popularity was reflected during the 2010 awards season. That year, he was nominated for three Teen Choice Awards. Derulo won two TCAs: "Choice R&B Track" for "In My Head" and "Choice R&B Album" for *Jason Derulo*. He was also nominated for two MTV Video Music Awards, two MTV Europe Music Awards, an ARIA Music Award, and an American Music Award. But Derulo's greatest success was yet to come.

Derulo pours his heart and soul into a performance in London, England, during his 2010 world tour.

CHAPTER
4

Different Directions

Jason Derulo spent the second half of 2010 and the first half of 2011 on tour. His Jason Derulo World Tour began in August 2010 with a sold-out show in London, England, and continued through Europe, the United States, Australia, and New Zealand. The tour made it clear that Derulo was truly popular all over the world.

After the tour ended, Derulo headed back to the recording studio. In 2011, Derulo recorded a song with Demi Lovato called "Together." The song appeared on her album, *Unbroken*. Derulo was busy with his own work as well. On September 27, 2011, his second album, *Future History*, was released. Derulo gave fans an inside look at the making of the album by posting a series of videos on his Web site.

Derulo was getting ready for another tour to support *Future History* when he had the frightening accident that broke a vertebra in his neck. Even though the tour had to be canceled, Derulo kept busy recording. He also returned to the stage as soon as he could. Just four and a half months after the accident, on May 22, 2012, Derulo performed on the eleventh season finale of the hit TV show *American Idol*.

Derulo ventured into other areas of the entertainment business. He decided to start his own record label with his manager. On July 9, 2012, he announced he had signed an Australian singer-songwriter named Arlene Zelina.

Along with being a singer, Derulo is also a talented dancer. He put those talents to use when he signed on as dance master for the first season of an Australian talent show called *Everybody Dance Now*. Unfortunately, the show did not do well and was cancelled after just four episodes. However, Derulo enjoyed his time as a judge and would like to do it again. He told the *Daily Record* he would love to be a judge or mentor on *The Voice* or another show like that. However, he had learned that being a judge was not all fun and games. "If the opportunity came up, I'd definitely want it, but you've got to be prepared for all that comes with it. It's hard breaking people's hearts. On one hand, you're making one person's dreams come true, on the other, you could be crushing someone else's dreams."

Derulo was back in the recording studio in 2013 to work on his third album, *Tattoos*, which was released on September 24, 2013. As he had done with his earlier albums, Derulo released several singles to iTunes and the radio well before the album came out. "The Other Side" was released on April 23, 2013, and climbed to number 18 on the *Billboard* Hot 100 chart. Next up was a hip-hop song called "Talk Dirty," which was released on July 28, 2013. This song

> *Derulo ventured into other areas of the entertainment business. He decided to start his own record label with his manager.*

Derulo performs live during the American Idol *Season 11 finale on May 22, 2012. It was his first performance after his neck injury.*

became a huge smash, reaching number 3 on the *Billboard* charts. As Derulo described the dance hit, "It's very out there, but it was so fun."

Derulo showed a more romantic side with his third single, "Marry Me," which was written for his girlfriend, Jordin Sparks. The song reached number 26 on the *Billboard* Hot 100 chart and was described as the world's "next top wedding tune" by PopCrush.com music critic Karen Lanza.

Originally, the full *Tattoos* album was not released in the United States. Six months after it was released in other parts of the world, Derulo made a big announcement. He would be releasing a new album in the United States that would include seven songs from *Tattoos* along with four newly recorded songs. The new album was called *Talk Dirty* and was released on April 15, 2014. The album entered the *Billboard* 200 album chart at number 4 and sold 44,000 copies in its first week. By the end of May 2014, the album had sold more than 90,000 copies.

> **With a new album to promote, it was time for Derulo to go back on the road. The Tattoos World Tour began in February with a show in Paris, France.**

With a new album to promote, it was time for Derulo to go back on the road. The Tattoos World Tour began in February with a show in Paris, France. The tour continued through Europe before moving on to New Zealand, Australia, and the United States. As always, Derulo worked hard to bring his dynamic music and performances to audiences all over the world.

"Talk Dirty" was one of the most popular songs of 2014. Derulo promoted the song during an appearance at a Lucky Strikes in New York City on April 17, 2014.

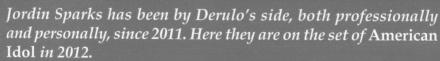
Jordin Sparks has been by Derulo's side, both professionally and personally, since 2011. Here they are on the set of American Idol in 2012.

Giving Back and Moving Forward

*O*ver the past few years, Jason Derulo's career has turned into a dream come true. The same is true of his personal life. In 2011, Derulo met Jordin Sparks. Sparks is also a pop singer and had won *American Idol* in 2007. The two did not connect when they first met because both were dating other people at the time, but later they got together and have been close ever since.

Derulo and Sparks had a big challenge to face when they first began dating because they lived on opposite sides of the country. Derulo lived in Florida while Sparks' hometown was in Arizona. To bridge the distance, the two traveled often to be together, and Sparks spent a lot of time at Derulo's Miami home.

Meeting Sparks changed Derulo's life. "My relationship with Jordin has made a huge difference to my life," he told Britain's *Daily Record*. "Jordin came in and turned my world upside down and you know what, it's an awesome world. . . . There's nothing like having that special someone in your corner. It keeps you going."

Derulo needed all of Sparks' help after Derulo broke his neck in 2012. During his recovery, Derulo had to rely on his family for help with just about everything. Sparks became one of his strongest champions. "She was a huge support system through my whole injury," Derulo told the *Daily Record*. "She was one of the backbones that kept me going through the recovery."

> *Religion is important to Derulo. He prays every day and says that his faith has given him the confidence to achieve great things.*

Derulo has shown his love for Sparks in several big ways. In 2014, he gave Sparks 10,000 orange (her favorite color) roses for Valentine's Day. After Sparks got over her surprise, the couple donated most of the roses to local hospitals to cheer up patients. Derulo has also recorded with Sparks and was featured on her single, "Before It Breaks," which was released in August 2013. Derulo wrote and recorded his own song, "Marry Me," for Sparks, although the two are not presently engaged.

Religion is important to Derulo. He prays every day and says that his faith has given him the confidence to achieve great things. Derulo also believes in giving back. He knows that he was very fortunate to grow up in a family that had the financial resources to send him to performing arts schools and support his dream of being a performer. Now that he is a success, Derulo tries to help other young people find their way.

Because of his Haitian background, Derulo was especially eager to help after a devastating earthquake

Derulo believes in helping others, especially young people and people in need. So it's no surprise that he entertained fans by performing at a student talent show at a school in Miami, Florida.

struck Haiti in 2010. Derulo donated thousands of dollars to Haitian relief efforts without asking for a lot of publicity for his generosity. He also performed at benefit concerts for the victims, including a telethon called *SOS Saving Ourselves: Help for Haiti* which aired on several music channels as well as being streamed live online in February, 2010.

In 2010, *Beatweek* Magazine asked Derulo if he felt responsibility for helping the victims of the Haitian earthquake. Derulo replied, "I feel such a large responsibility. I am young, but that doesn't mean that I can just sit back and let things happen the way that they're

One of Derulo's idols is Michael Jackson. Along with his singing and dancing talents, Derulo often copies Jackson's fashion statements by wearing flashy outfits like this one to events.

happening." He went on to share that he was on his way to entertain at a local school that had taken in several students who had lost family members in the disaster. "I'm going to the school just to bring a little ray of sunshine."

Derulo has big plans for the future and they don't just include singing, dancing, and recording. He would also like to act. In 2010, Derulo appeared in an MTV-produced dance film called *Turn the Beat Around*, and in 2012 he guest-starred in a US television show called *State of Georgia* with Raven-Symone. "I can't wait to do some more acting," he told the *Daily Record*. "It's been a life-long passion of mine. I went to college to study acting, actually, so I've always been really into it. I wouldn't mind being in an action flick."

At just twenty-five years old, Jason Derulo has made many of his dreams come true. But he still has many big dreams to fill.

At just twenty-five years old, Jason Derulo has made many of his dreams come true. But he still has many big dreams to fill. Derulo told *USA Today* that Michael Jackson is his biggest influence. "I only hope to impact the world a fraction of how he has," Derulo said. This is a dream that Derulo could very likely achieve.

1989   Jason Joel Desrouleaux is born on September 21.

1997   Derulo writes his first song and begins attending a performing arts school.

2005   Derulo begins writing songs for major rap and hip-hop artists.

2006   Derulo graduates from the American Musical and Dramatic Academy in New York City; he wins the grand prize on the television show *Showtime at the Apollo*; he meets music producer J.R. Rotem

2009   Derulo releases his first single, "Whatcha Say," followed by "In My Head."

2010   Derulo's first album, *Jason Derulo*, is released; he tours with Lady Gaga; he wins two Teen Choice Awards; he begins a world tour.

2011   Derulo records with Demi Lovato; he releases his second album, *Future History*; he begins dating singer Jordin Sparks.

2012   Derulo breaks a vertebra in his neck while rehearsing for an upcoming tour; Derulo returns to performing on *American Idol* on May 22.

2013   Derulo releases his third album, *Tattoos*, featuring the hit single "Talk Dirty."

2014   Derulo releases the album *Talk Dirty* in the United States; he begins a world tour.

DISCOGRAPHY

2010	*Jason Derulo*	2013	*Tattoos*
2011	*Future History*	2014	*Talk Dirty*

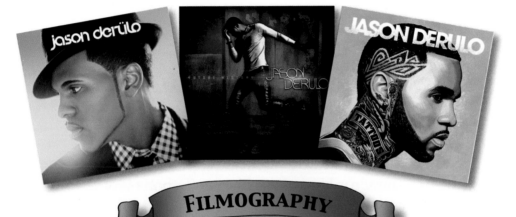

FILMOGRAPHY

2010	*Turn the Beat Around*
2010	*Everybody Dance Now*
2012	*State of Georgia*

FURTHER READING

Books
Gogerly, Liz. *Pop Stars*. New York: PowerKids Press, 2012.

On the Internet
Jason Derulo
    http://www.jasonderulo.com
Jason Derulo Biography/Billboard
    http://www.billboard.com/artist/304245/jason-derulo/
    biography

Works Consulted
Chen, Joyce. "Jason Derulo Fractures Neck, Almost Paralyzed
    While Training for Upcoming Shows, Cancels World Tour."
    The New York Daily News, January 6, 2012. http://www.
    nydailynews.com/gossip/jason-derulo-fractures-neck-
    paralyzed-training-upcoming-shows-cancels-tour-article-
    1.1001974?localLinksEnabled=false/
Code, Bill. "Interview with Jonathan 'JR' Rotem." HitQuarters.
    com, April 5, 2010. http://www.hitquarters.com/index.
    php3?page=intrview/2010/April5_0_0_1.html
Coster, Alice. "Arlene Rides the Tube to Fame." *The Herald Sun*.
    http://www.heraldsun.com.au/entertainment/music/
    arlene-rides-the-tube-to-fame/story-e6frf9hf-1226420514237/
"Jason Derulo Breaks Neck While Practicing Stunt, Cancels
    Upcoming Tour." PerezHilton. http://perezhilton.com/2012-
    01-06-jason-derulo-breaks-neck-and-cancels-upcoming-tour/
Lanza, Karen. "Jason Derulo, 'Marry Me' — Song Review."
    PopCrush.com. http://popcrush.com/jason-derulo-marry-
    me-song-review/
Lewis, Pete. "Jason Derulo: Watcha Think?" Blues & Soul.com.
    http://www.bluesandsoul.com/feature/484/jason_derulo_
    watcha_think/

Lopez, Korina. "On the Verge: Future Star Jason Derulo Tips His Hat to the Past." *USA Today*, March 15, 2010. http://usatoday30.usatoday.com/life/music/news/2010-03-15-otv15_ST_N.htm

Palmer, Bill. "Jason Derulo: The Beatweek Interview." *Beatweek Magazine*, March 9, 2010. http://beatweek-com.wpengine.netdna-cdn.com/magazine/BeatweekMagazineIssue65.pdf

"R&B Star Jason Derulo on How Breaking His Neck Changed His Entire Outlook on Life." *The Daily Record*. http://www.dailyrecord.co.uk/entertainment/celebrity-interviews/rb-star-jason-derulo-how-2364829/

Rettig, James. "Jason Derulo Announces 'Tattoos' Album, Releases 'Talk Dirty' Track with 2 Chainz." Billboard.com. http://www.billboard.com/articles/columns/pop-shop/4320321/jason-derulo-announces-tattoos-album-releases-talk-dirty-track/

"Sarah Murdoch, Jason Derulo & Kelly Rowland Join 'Everybody Dance Now.' " Throng.com. http://www.throng.com.au/2012/06/sarah-murdoch-jason-derulo-kelly-rowland-join-everybody-dance-now/

Vena, Jocelyn. "Jason Derulo Says Lady Gaga 'Forced Me to Step My Game Up.' " MTV.com. http://www.mtv.com/news/1629430/jason-derulo-says-lady-gaga-forced-me-to-step-my-game-up/

INDEX